HARRY BERAN

BETEL-CHEWING EQUIPMENT OF EAST NEW GUINEA

GW00568229

SHIRE ETHNOGRAPHY

Cover photograph
Two spatulas with a human figure, squatting and facing forward, one holding a drum.
Left: Type 5, wood, length 270 mm (10⅝ inches). (MM 1944 Oc.2. 1900, ex Beasley
Collection.) Right: Type 6, wood, length 282 mm (11⅛ inches). (MM 1944. Oc.2. 1901,
ex Beasley Collection.) (Photographs: Museum of Mankind.)

British Library Cataloguing in Publication Data
Beran, Harry.
Betel-chewing Equipment of East New Guinea.
— (Shire ethnography; 8).
1. Papua New Guinea. Massim. Betel.
Mastication.
I. Title.
394. 1'2.
ISBN 0-85263-969-4.

For Clare,
who collects people.

Published by
SHIRE PUBLICATIONS LTD
Cromwell House, Church Street, Princes Risborough,
Aylesbury, Bucks HP17 9AJ, UK

Series Editor: Bryan Cranstone

ISBN 0 85263 969 4

First published 1988

Set in 11 point Times and printed in Great Britain by
C. I. Thomas & Sons (Haverfordwest) Ltd,
Press Buildings, Merlins Bridge, Haverfordwest, Dyfed.

Contents

Acknowledgements

Many debts of gratitude have been incurred on the way: to Chiefs Narubutau and Uwelasi for interviews in 1982 and 1983 and to Chief Tolosi for an interview in 1987; to John Kasaipwalova and Jerome Koubuli who translated in 1982-3 and 1987 respectively and gave independent information themselves; to the other Massim informants mentioned in the text who were interviewed in 1987; to Cecil Abel, Shirley Campbell, Peter Hallinan and Ralph Lawton who have shared their knowledge with me on a number of occasions; to Bryan Cranstone, Antonia Lovelace, Anthony Tynan, Jim Specht, Lissant Bolton, Michael Quinnel, Graeme Pretty, Dimitri Anson and, most of all, Dorota Starzecka, among museum staff; to public and private collections for permission to illustrate some of their objects; and to Beverley Davis, Leo Fleischmann, Clare Harding, Radomir Joura, Anthony J. P. Meyer, John Schuster and Susan Simons for various assistance.

Special thanks are due to Keith Fyfe for his splendid drawings for this book.

4

List of illustrations

1
Betel chewing

Betel chewing is a central part of life in East New Guinea. Children start chewing when only a few years old. Adults chew when they make love, meet friends, work in the gardens, attend feasts and during canoe voyages. In Dobu, betel nuts are placed in the hands of a corpse for the guardian of the place of the dead so he will let the spirit pass.

Betel is chewed by about a tenth of the world's population in an area stretching from East Africa across India, Sri Lanka, southern China, mainland South-east Asia, Indonesia and the Philippines to New Guinea and nearby islands. It is a mild stimulant which reduces hunger pangs and produces feelings of good humour, well-being and an increased capacity for work. Chewing also improves the odour of the breath, increases the flow of saliva and colours it and the teeth red.

The ingredients and implements used in betel chewing vary in different cultures. In East New Guinea only the three essential ingredients are consumed. These are the so-called 'betel-nut' (the seed of the areca palm), the fruit or leaf of the betel plant (a climber) and mineral lime (burnt coral). The commonly used but potentially misleading phrase 'betel-nut' will be retained in this book to refer to the areca nut. This is legitimate provided the phrase is understood to mean 'the nut which is chewed with betel' rather than 'the nut produced by the betel plant'.

What contribution the ingredients of the betel chew make to its effects is not entirely clear. It appears that the euphoria is caused by the nicotine-like properties of the alkaloids in the betel-nut and that these alkaloids are released from the nut by the lime. The increase in salivation and the pleasant mouth odour seem also to be due to the interaction of the nut with the lime. Chewers report that the saliva is reddest and that the chew tastes best when all three ingredients are used together.

The utensils used in betel chewing in East New Guinea are amongst the finest Melanesian works of art. The equipment consists of lime containers, lime spatulas to convey the lime from the container to the mouth, mortars and pestles to crush the betel-nuts and baskets in which these utensils are stored or carried. Most limepots carry superb burnt-in designs and finely woven stoppers. Betel-nut mortars are carved in imitation of canoes, drums and human figures or are decorated with animal designs. Pestles too are adorned with various motifs. The finest carvings, however, are the lime spatulas. Most carry representations of human figures, animals, plants or artefacts. The best spatulas and mortars are masterpieces of miniature sculpture.

East New Guinea, for the purpose of this book, refers to the Massim culture district of New Guinea. This district coincides approximately with the Milne Bay Province of Papua New Guinea (plate 1). One island group in the province, the Trobriands, is famous through the books of Bronislaw Malinowski, one of the founders of modern anthropology, who did his most important fieldwork there. Other islands, such as Misima, are known to the outside world as gold-mining areas. 'Massim', the name of the area as a culture region, appears to be a corruption of Misima. Milne Bay, the source of the name 'Milne Bay Province', entered world history as the location of the Second World War battle of Milne Bay, in which the American Navy defeated the Japanese. At the beginning of the twentieth century the area was inhabited by about 38,000 people.

Massim artefacts have been collected since at least the beginning of the nineteenth century. The earliest surviving collection, made by Owen Stanley's Rattlesnake expedition in 1849, is in the Museum of Mankind (plates 55, 67).

Between the 1870s and 1930s thousands of Massim betel-chewing utensils were collected by missionaries, government officials, anthropologists, travellers and others. Most of these have been deposited in Western museums.

By the 1890s enough spatulas were available in the West for A. C. Haddon to publish a classification of their designs (1894). In the twentieth century production standards declined rapidly. Malinowski's collections in the Museum of Mankind, London, the Robert H. Lowie Museum of Anthropology, Berkeley, and the National Museum of Victoria, Melbourne, made in the 1910s, contain few outstanding pieces; the collections of Jüptner (private), of Lawton in the South Australian Museum, Adelaide, and the National Museum of Papua New Guinea, and of Gerrits in the Queensland Museum, Brisbane, made in the 1950s and 1960s, contain few old pieces and only a small range of designs. (Museums are sometimes referred to by abbreviations; see chapter 7.) After the Second World War new spatula designs were introduced for the tourist trade. Some are shown in Germer (1965), especially figures 21-3. These tourist pieces are not dealt with in this book. Few old betel-chewing utensils are left in the Massim area. In the 1980s Rossel Island seems to be the only place where traditional spatula designs are still carved. Elsewhere other objects, often of Western origin, are commonly used as spatulas and lime

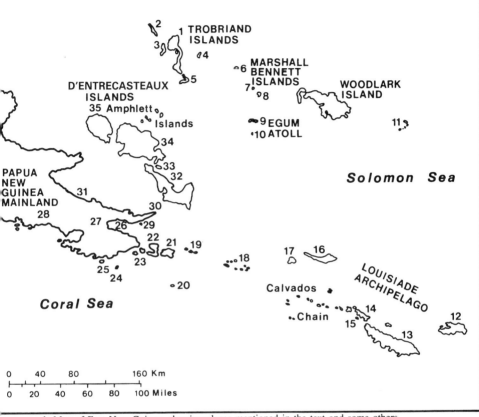

1. Map of East New Guinea, showing places mentioned in the text and some others.

1. Kiriwina Island
2. Tuma Island
3. Keileuna Island
4. Kitava Island
5. Vakuta Island
6. Iwa Island
7. Kwaiawata Island
8. Gawa Island
9. Yanaba Island
10. Egum Islet
11. Budibudi Islands
12. Rossel Island
13. Tagula Island
14. Pana Tinane Island
15. Wanim Island
16. Misima Island
17. Paneati Island
18. Conflict Group
19. Engineer Group
20. Teste Island
21. Basilaki Island
22. Sideia Island
23. Samarai Island
24. Brumer Island
25. Suau Island (South Cape)
26. Milne Bay
27. Buhutu Valley
28. Daga people
29. Killerton Islands
30. East Cape
31. Wedau Village
32. Normanby Island
33. Dobu Island
34. Fergusson Island
35. Goodenough Island

containers, though in the Trobriands chiefs still prefer to use cassowary bone spatulas (plate 2). Simply carved mortars and pestles are still made throughout the area as no Western substitutes are available.

This book offers a typology of spatulas in terms of what their handles represent. It is based on the inspection of about 3700 pieces held in public collections in London, Oxford, Cambridge, Liverpool, Edinburgh, Aberdeen, Dublin, Buffalo, Cambridge (Massachusetts), Chicago, Dresden, Leipzig, Vienna, Budapest, Paris, Sydney, Brisbane, Canberra, Melbourne, Adelaide, Auckland, Dunedin, Osaka and Port Moresby, listed in chapter 7. Smaller collections were also inspected at the Hunterian Museum and the Museum and Art Gallery in Glasgow, the Ethnographic Museum in Prague, the University of Queensland Anthropology Museum, the National Gallery of Victoria in Melbourne, the Macleay Museum at Sydney University and the National Museum, Wellington. Another four hundred spatulas are known to the author from private collections and published illustrations. The substantial public collections in Berkeley and Stockholm have not been inspected, nor the smaller collections in numerous other American and European museums. Hence, the present typology is based on inspection of about three-quarters of the spatulas known to exist.

A typology of mortars, pestles, limepots and baskets is also offered. Far fewer of these exist than spatulas and there is less variety of design.

The following collections have been especially useful in establishing the precise origin of some types of utensil because the place of collection seems to be reliably recorded: P. G. Black, formed 1886-1916 (Buffalo Museum of Science); G. Brown, 1890-1905 (National Museum of Ethnology, Osaka); S. B. Fellows, 1891-1901 (Australian National Gallery, Canberra); Cooke Daniels, 1904 (Museum of Mankind, London); K. Verebelyi, 1910-20 (Museum of Ethnography, Budapest); B. Malinowski, 1914-20 (Museum of Mankind, Robert H. Lowie Museum of Anthropology, National Museum of Victoria).

The information offered below is written in the ethnographic present, except where inappropriate.

2
The people of East New Guinea

People and culture

The Massim people are island traders happily dubbed by Malinowski the 'Argonauts of the Western Pacific'. Most live on the steep volcanic or low-lying coral islands off the easternmost tip of New Guinea, the rest on the mainland itself. From most islands the next inhabited island is visible on a clear day.

The material culture of the people of Milne Bay Province, with the exception of the Rossel Island and Daga people, is sufficiently homogeneous and stylistically different from that of neighbouring peoples to allow it to be spoken of as a distinctive Massim material culture. The Massim are among the minority of New Guineans who speak Melanesian (Austronesian) languages and have a matrilineal social structure (except for the Goodenough people, who are patrilineal). Their material culture is extremely rich. Among their finest products are large overseas trading canoes, shell ornaments, clay pots, ebony and blackpalm weapons, the famous Trobriand war-shields and betel-chewing utensils. Pottery and basket work is done by women, wood carving and most shell work by men. Every man may carve, but in the Trobriands certain objects are made only by master carvers (for example, chiefly houseboards, *kula* canoe boards and some lime spatulas). In the Milne Bay area the carving of important canoes belongs to some families by hereditary right. Wood is cut and shaped with stone- and shell-headed axes and adzes, engraved with bone, teeth and obsidian and polished with sting-ray skins, leaves and boars' tusks. The holes in the shell discs used for various ornaments are made with pump drills. (In the early 1900s metal blades and nails increasingly replaced traditional tools.)

Communities are divided into three to twelve clans. Each clan has up to four totems, one each drawn from bird, fish, animal and plant species. Some of the totemic creatures are carved on artefacts, but such carving is not restricted to those whose totems they are and there is little evidence that they are carved because they are totems.

The Massim sustain life primarily through agriculture and fishing. Yams, taros, bananas and coconuts are the main crops, while in the south sago is also important. Wild fruits, sugar cane, breadfruit, pigs, bush hens, turtles and crocodiles are among the many other foods consumed.

Death is a major ceremonial occasion. It is marked by a series of important distributions of valuables and food. Other major life transitions (birth, adulthood, marriage) are accompanied by little or no ritual. The spirits of the dead go to live on a particular island or mountain near their former homes. In the Trobriands, for example, they go to Tuma Island where they lead a blissful subterranean existence. From Tuma they return once a year to take part in the harvest festival, *milamala.* There they receive offerings, sometimes show themselves to the living, but do not influence them much for better or worse. The Massim also believe in non-human spirits, which inhabit trees, swamps, springs and rocky areas and are generally thought to be malevolent or indifferent to humans. There are few cults involving supernatural beings, the cult of the ambisexual divinity of war, Yaboaine, in the D'Entrecasteaux, being one exception.

There is much localised and specialised manufacture and therefore utilitarian trade occurs between island communities. Some of it takes place on voyages undertaken for the ceremonial exchange of shell valuables (the *kula,* see below). Canoes, clay pots, wooden bowls, axe- and adze-blades, pigs, food and betel-nuts are among the most common items of trade. Ceremonial greenstone axe-blades, shell discs mounted on wooden or turtleshell handles (plates 56, 57), whalebone lime spatulas (plate 69), shell necklaces, shell armbands and pigs can be used as payment for substantial items such as canoes.

Betel-chewing utensils are also traded widely. This trade includes the export of spatulas from Kitava to Kiriwina, from the Trobriands to the D'Entrecasteaux and to Tubetube (Engineer Group), from Wedau to Goodenough and from Rossel Island to Tagula; that of limepots from Kiriwina to Kitava and from the Trobriands to the D'Entrecasteaux; and that of three-tiered baskets from the Trobriands to Goodenough.

Trade between the Massim and their neighbours appears to be limited. However, along the south coast of New Guinea, Massim armshells are traded all the way to the Motu around Port Moresby. In the nineteenth century shell-disc necklaces may also have been imported by the Massim from the Motu, before the latter ceased manufacture.

The Massim believe that most, if not all, human objectives can be fostered or frustrated by magic. It is used to increase the fertility of the soil, the seaworthiness of canoes, the power of wood carvers and of the weapons they make, to control the weather, to make *kula* partners yield desired items, to inspire love, to make sick and to kill. In the Trobriands, male sorcerers, called *bwaga'u,* and female witches, called *mulukwausi,* are especially feared. *Bwaga'u* can kill by inducing a deadly disease in their victim, *mulukwausi* by removing the internal organs from them. The witches eat these organs,

2. Chief Siyoula of Lobua Village, Kiriwina, with cassowary bone lime spatula (type 41) and plain limepot. The spatula and pot decorated with white cowrie shells indicate their owner's chiefly rank. (Photograph: Harry Beran, 1969.)

sometimes after hiding them temporarily. The only remedy against attack by a sorcerer or witch is to hire another *bwaga'u* to counter the death magic or another *mulukwausi* to find and restore the missing organs. *Mulukwausi* are especially feared by *kula* travellers since they prey on shipwrecked mariners.

The following events illustrate how lime spatulas can be used in black magic (Fortune, 1963, pages 161-3). A Dobuan sorcerer was deeply insulted by a fellow Dobuan, who accused him of having no new garden food because he spent too much time at sea (doing *kula*?). Later the sorcerer put a spell on his spatula, followed the other man into the latter's garden and, once there, burst on him with a sorcerer's scream. The gardener collapsed and the sorcerer used his spatula, without actually touching the victim's body, to remove his entrails, heart and lungs. The sorcerer charmed his spatula once more, made the victim rise and told him to go. The gardener went back to his village raving and calling for his missing organs. Within a day he lay dead.

Though the material culture of the inhabitants of the Milne Bay Province is distinct from those of neighbouring areas, a further distinction can be made between the artefacts and social customs of the northern and southern parts of the province. The difference between the canoes, weapons, shields and drums of the two areas is illustrated in Newton (1975) and Beran (1980). This book shows that, while some types of spatula are made throughout the province, other types are made only in the north and yet others only in the south.

In socio-political organisation too the Trobriands and Marshall Bennetts differ from the southern islands and the mainland. In the former, sub-clan membership determines hereditary social rank and the right to rule. Village groups in the northern half of Kiriwina form alliances around the chief of one village. The chief of Omarakana Village, always of the highest ranking Tabalu sub-clan, has the highest status of all. The village alliances are partly based on polygyny, with the senior chief in the alliance drawing ten or more wives from the other villages in the alliance and receiving annual tributes of yams from his wives' relatives. On Woodlark and in the southern Massim, influence is not based on hereditary rank but wielded by men who have gained repute through personal accomplishment. In these areas polygyny is rare and involves only two or three wives.

The size of settlements tends to be larger in the north. In the Trobriands some villages are inhabited by hundreds of people. The buildings in some of these villages are arranged as an inner circle of yam stores surrounded by an outer circle of dwellings, all facing a central plaza used for dancing and burials. Most settlements in the south are clusters of hamlets with only a few dozen inhabitants.

The Rossel Islanders in the extreme south-east of the province and the Daga people, who live in the rugged mountains of the mainland, only partly share the Massim culture characteristics. They are the only people in the province who speak Papuan or non-Austronesian languages. The Rossel Islanders also believe in a hierarchy of gods unknown elsewhere in the province and make some canoes which, stylistically, are not Massim. However, like almost all Massim, they have matrilineal descent and, in the western part of the island, make sailing canoes and lime spatulas which, stylistically, are clearly Massim (plate 49).

The kula

Most of the island communities are linked through the *kula* exchange cycle in which shell-disc necklaces (*soulava*) and shell armbands (*mwali*) are ceremonially exchanged. The necklace discs are made on Vakuta and in the Louisiades from *chama* shells and the armbands in the Trobriands and on Woodlark from *conus* shells. The southernmost islands of the Louisiades do not participate in the *kula* but make shell-disc necklaces which can become *soulava*.

In the *kula* exchange the necklaces travel clockwise and the armbands counter-clockwise around a giant ring of island communities. Individual pieces, as a rule, take two to ten years to complete the round. The thousands of ornaments in the *kula* are ranked in categories of value. Their value depends partly on their age, patina and history and partly on the size of the armband and the length and colour of the necklace. Over time some items, especially lesser ones, leak out of the system. Others increase in value through further processing (especially of the necklace shell discs) and the acquisition of patina and history. The most valuable items are individually named, known to have gone round the whole circle many times and renowned throughout the area.

As a rule only men *kula*. They sail together on annual expeditions to their individual partners on other islands with whom they can have lifelong exchange relationships. Some of the tension of *kula* arises from the exchange of armshells and necklaces not being simultaneous. Thus, a party of Dobuans will travel to the Trobriands to obtain armshells. In the next sailing season, Trobrianders will travel to Dobu and each Dobuan who received an armshell will be expected to give his Trobriand partner a necklace of comparable value. A lime spatula and charmed betel-nuts may be given to the *kula* partner to induce him to *kula*. *Kula* pieces, especially famous ones, must be kept in circulation. Individuals hold them only temporarily. However, since *kula* is competitive, participants strive to hold for a time the most valuable and the greatest number of pieces possible.

Kula provides scope for acquiring influence, fame and even a kind of immortality. It can also be fatally dangerous, for those with whom one *kulas* on other islands are not only partners but also competitors and, sometimes, not only hosts but also foes. A number of Trobriand sailing parties are said to have been caught and eaten by the Dobuans.

A number of reasons, not mutually exclusive, have been suggested as to why the Massim *kula*. Perhaps they *kula* because they value the personal relationships and inter-island communication involved; or because it provides the opportunity competitively to acquire prestige and immortality; or because it is a surrogate for warfare and thereby permits the utilitarian trade essential among the islands because of their different resources. At most, however, *kula* is only a partial surrogate for war, since violent conflict between island communities is not uncommon. On Kiriwina there is also warfare between villages of the same island. (Warfare was suppressed by the colonial administration from the end of the nineteenth century but *kula* continues strongly in the 1980s.)

History and mythology

The first Westerners to visit the Massim area were Torres and Prado, who sighted Tagula and Basilaki Island in 1606. D'Entrecasteaux traversed the region in 1793. Owen Stanley (1849) and John Moresby (1873) captained important expeditions to the area. Whalers began to stop at some islands from the 1830s. Western commercial activities and Christian mission stations were introduced in the second half of the nineteenth century. The area was part of the British New Guinea Protectorate established in 1884 and received its first government station, at Samarai, in 1886.

Little is known about the history of the Massim before Western contact. There are prehistoric megalithic structures in the Trobriands and on Woodlark, and sites with anthropomorphic and geometric rock engravings, especially in the D'Entrecasteaux and on the mainland. Nothing is known about their age or origin. Pottery sherds, plentiful in deserted village sites, show that some of the islands have been inhabited for up to two thousand years and that significant changes in pottery design and trade have occurred during this period.

Trobrianders believe that humans led a fully social subterranean existence before they appeared on earth from caves. Waibadi, the paramount chief of Kiriwina, who died in 1987, could recite the names of his eighty predecessors. The myth of Tudava, known throughout the northern Massim area, explains the origin of some of the islands there and how they became populated. Tudava was the first man to emerge from the ground in Kiriwina. As other men emerged he gave them their totems. He created Kitava, the Marshall Bennetts and Woodlark by throwing stones in the sea. The Kiriwinans then populated these islands by sailing there in canoes (Malinowski, 1978, page 68). However, the Marshall Bennett people also have another myth according to which their original ancestors emerged from holes on their own islands (Seligman, 1910, pages 686-7).

Labai Village, in northern Kiriwina, is said to be the original village of that island. Tolosi, its chief in 1987, explains the origin and spread of betel chewing as follows. Dovana and his brother were among the first people to come out of Obuwaga cave near Labai. Dovana brought all the betel-chewing ingredients and utensils with him. One day Dovana asked his brother to get some fire from his hut. When his brother did not return for a long time, Dovana followed and found him making love to his (Dovana's) wife. On seeing this, he killed him with a spear. He took the corpse south and in every village he asked people to eat part of the corpse. Those who ate were rewarded with betel-nuts, but the people of most villages refused. So Dovana took the corpse and the betel-nuts to the D'Entrecasteaux. This explains why there are more betel-nuts in the D'Entrecasteaux than in the Trobriands. Dovana also took betel-nuts to Woodlark.

The Dobuans (Fortune, 1963, page 281) and the people of Wagawaga Village in Milne Bay (Seligman, 1910, page 422f) do not have subterranean origin myths. Nor do any other origin myths appear to have been recorded for the southern Massim.

3
Lime spatulas

The visual analysis of Massim betel-chewing utensils shows that most of them fall into distinctive design types. In this analysis, the object as a whole is examined rather than small parts of it and obvious representations such as humans, animals and artefacts are noted. Indeed, the typology offered is based on what the carvings represent, because so many of them carry images of things that are important in Massim life. This chapter presents a typology of spatula designs, the next a typology of mortars, pestles, limepots and the baskets in which they are carried.

Approximately eighty per cent of spatulas fall into visually distinctive types. For specimens of some types there is a considerable range of collection dates and recorded collection places. This suggests that some designs are traditional (that is, made by successive generations of carvers) and that they are carved in a number of different places. Research on museum collections provides strong evidence for the correctness of both suggestions. Field evidence fully confirms them. (See the comments on clapper-type spatulas below.)

A group of spatulas can be identified as a traditional design type by visual analysis if: their handles are more similar in design to each other than to those of other spatulas; there is, nevertheless, sufficient variation of design detail to suggest that a number of carvers made spatulas of the design identified; some of the specimens of the design group identified by the first two criteria show signs of having been used as lime spatulas by a betel/saliva deposit on their blades.

The clappers illustrated (plates 18-21) meet these criteria and show how a traditional type of lime spatula can be identified by visual analysis. Though there is considerable variation in the design of clappers they are more similar to each other than to other spatulas.

Forty-five types of spatula, listed below, have been identified by visual analysis. Information gathered in the field has also been used to interpret some types, to develop categories of types and to assign types to categories. For example, visual analysis is sufficient to identify spatulas with a 'dart-shaped' handle as a distinct type (type 23, plate 43). However, only fieldwork can reveal that the handle represents the *bulabula* flower and should therefore be included in the category of plant motif handles. As this last example shows, some of the visually distinctive types of spatula are also recognised as distinctive by Massim people.

The following list indicates, for each spatula type, its name in

Kiriwinan, if known, and the approximate number of specimens located. The list is followed by comments on most of the types and an illustration of the most attractive or otherwise most interesting specimen of each type. The general word for lime spatula is *kena* in the Trobriands, *ghena* in Tagula and *ch:aa* in Rossel Island.

TYPOLOGY OF LIME SPATULAS

I. Human figure motif handles
1. Figure squatting in profile, 350, plate 3.
2. Figure squatting on its feet, 35, plate 4.
3. Figure sitting on top of the blade with legs down its side, 11, plate 5.
4. Figure squatting with curve at back, 15, plates 6, 7.
5. Figure squatting, facing forward, 45, plate 8, cover.
6. Figure squatting, facing forward with a drum in its hands, 7, cover.
7. Figure squatting, facing forward, with limbs carved separate from the body, 40, plate 9.
8. Figure squatting, splayed, 30, plate 10.
9. Figure standing, facing forward, 25, plate 11.
10. Larger figure behind smaller figure, 6, plate 12.
11. Mother holding baby, 4, plate 13.
12. Two figures addorsed in profile, 55, plate 14.
13. One figure squatting on top of another squatting figure, 13, plate 15.

II. Animal motif handles
14. Clapper, *takakupwana,* 530, plates 18-21.
15. Snake facing into open jaws.
    a. Handle comes to point at top, 150, plate 24.
    b. Handle topped by band, 35, plate 25.
    c. Handle topped with bird, 80, plate 26.
    d. Handle topped with asymmetrical design, 13, plate 27.
    e. Handle topped with single squatting figure, 60 (not illustrated).
    f. Handle topped with two addorsed figures squatting in profile, 50, plate 28.
16. Curved lines connecting two concentric circles, 13, plate 31.
17. Fish and bird, 55, plate 32.
18. Unidentified animal (? *sibini*), 14, plate 33.
19. Bird, highly stylised, with long beak, 12 plate 34.
20. Praying mantis, 6, plate 35.

21. Unidentified animal with long snout and long ears, 3, plate 36.
22. Bar with rows of birds on both sides, 10, plate 37.

III. Plant motif handles
23. Flower, *tabulabula*, 60, plate 43.
24. Disc-shaped, *taubwara* (and *takubwana*), 60, plates 44, 45.

IV. Artefact motif handles
25. Canoe or canoe prow, 40, plates 46-8.
26. Canoe tip, 60, plates 49-52.
27. Canoe motif, *tanagega*, 40, plate 53.
28. Canoe steering paddle, *takuriga*, 3, plate 54.
29. Crescent-shaped.
    a. In wood, 25, plate 55.
    b. In turtleshell, rare, plate 56.
30. Imitation of whalebone spatula.
    a. In turtleshell, rare, plate 58.
    b. In wood, 30, plate 59.

V. Non-representational handles and handles with unidentified motifs
31. Loop, 95, plate 60.
32. Loop with central bar, 8, plate 61.
33. Ring, 10, plate 62.
34. Ring with interior projection, 7, plate 63.
35. Bar, square in cross-section, 70, plate 64.
36. Flat, oblong, 80?, plate 65.
37. Long, flat with rounded top, 70?, plate 66.
38. Oval, with bar pointing into a crescent carved in relief, 3, plate 67.
39. Rounded end with snake carved in relief, 7, plate 68.
40. Rounded end tapering towards tip (whale or dugong bone), *bosu*, rare, plate 69.
41. Tapering form (cassowary bone), *gesuwali*, rare, plate 2.
42. Tapering or straight spatulate shape (human bone), rare, plate 70.

VI. Non-representational double-purpose spatulas
43. Betel mortar in handle (blackpalm), 11, plate 71.
44. Betel mortar in handle (ebony), 40, plate 72.
45. Betel pestle in handle, 10, plate 73.

Human figure motifs

Spatulas with human figure handles are one of the three most common types, the others being spatulas of types 14 and 15. However, Shirley Campbell suggests that the wealth of specimens of these types may be partly due to their popularity with collectors rather than with original users.

Human figure spatulas can be used by magicians for protection on *kula* trips. The magician can call on a spirit *(tokwai)* to inhabit the figure on the spatula and protect its owner while asleep. A spatula with two figures may belong to a man who can call on two *tokwai* to protect him. (Information from Chief Narubutau.)

Spatulas with anthropomorphic handles are divided into types depending on whether one or two figures are carved, according to the position of the figure relative to the blade and according to the figure's posture. Thus, in single-figure types 1-4 (plates 3-6), the squatting figure faces sideways, while in types 5-9 (cover and plates 8-11), it faces forward. Among the figures squatting sideways, some have arms and legs in mirror image (type 1, plate 3), some squat on their feet (type 2, plate 4), some have legs hanging down below the top of the blade (type 3, plate 5) and some have a crescent-shaped design at the back (type 4, plates 6-7). Amongst the figures squatting facing forward, some have the limbs carved in the same way as type 1, that is, partly forward of the trunk and close together (type 5, plate 8). Some figures that squat facing forward carry a drum (type 6, cover). Other figures that squat facing forward have the limbs carved beside and free from the trunk (type 7, plate 9). Others, again, squat in a completely splayed position (type 8, plate 10). Finally, there are handles with a standing figure (type 9, plate 11). Four types of handle with two figures are distinguished. Some have a small figure in front of a larger one (type 10, plate 12), some a figure holding a baby (type 11, plate 13), some two addorsed figures (type 12, plate 14) and some have one squatting figure on top of another (type 13, plate 15). Some very fine anthropomorphic handle spatulas seem to be unique. Among these are the pieces in plates 16 and 17. The figure in plate 16 squats in a more relaxed pose than is usual, with its hands around its knees.

Quite often the figures on the handles are carved with a disc or cap-like object on their heads (plate 13). If, as seems likely, the figure in plate 13 is a mother with her baby, the disc could represent the head cover which nursing mothers wear in the Trobriands. Narubutau suggests that, on some pieces, the head cover may represent a human hair wig which bald men wear. As these remarks show, much Massim carving cries out for speculative interpretation. Spatulas of type 4

3. Spatula with human figure, squatting in profile (type 1). Wood. Length approximately 230 mm (9 inches). Collected by P. G. Black in the Trobriands, 1886-1916. (BMS C12368. Photograph: BMS.)

4. Spatula with human figure, squatting in profile on its feet (type 2). Wood. Length 300 mm (11¾ inches). (Michael Ball Collection. Photograph: Michael Ball.)

5. Spatula with human figure, sitting in profile on top of the blade with legs down its side (type 3). Ebony, betel-stained. Collected by the Reverend J. R. Andrews on Misima, before 1923. (SAM A12394. Photograph: Harry Beran.)

6. Spatula with human figure, squatting in profile with a curved design behind it (type 4). Ebony. Length 228 mm (9 inches). (Author's collection. Photograph: Radomir Joura.)

7. Rear view of curved design behind squatting figure on a spatula of type 4. Wood. (AMS E60800. Photograph: Ric Bolzan.)

8. Spatula with human figure, squatting facing forward, prominent male sex (type 5). Ebony. (Mme Marc de Monbrison Collection. Photograph: Mme Marc de Monbrison.)

9. Spatula with human figure, squatting facing forward, with limbs carved free from body (type 7). Tongue extended to chest. Brown wood. Length 248 mm (9¾ inches); most of blade missing. (Author's collection. Photograph: Radomir Joura.)

10. Spatula with human figure squatting in splayed position, facing forward (type 8). Wood. (Friede Collection. Photograph: Anthony J. P. Meyer.)

11. Spatula with human figure standing facing forward (type 9). Wood. Length 318 mm (12½ inches). (UMC 1955.250, donated by executors of Lady des Voeux. Photograph: UMC.)

illustrate the dangers of it. It is tempting to interpret the design at the back of the figure in plate 6 as a rain cape, which Kiriwinans make from pandanus leaves to protect their heads and shoulders. Narubutau, however, has interpreted another specimen of this type as portraying the queen on playing-cards!

Plate 17 shows a figure with its tongue extended to its chest. The portrayal of such an extended tongue is rare in Massim figurative carving. Quite a few other pieces have just the tip of the tongue showing between the lips (for example, those on the cover). Of the six specimens located with a small figure in front of a larger figure (type 10), one (MM 1944 Oc.2. 1904) has a large figure with a penis. It, therefore, must not be assumed that this type represents a mother and her child. Only four specimens of the maternity type 11 have been located. They have been classified as a traditional type despite their rarity, because they seem to have been made by at least three different carvers.

Different carving styles can be distinguished among figurative spatulas, ranging from the naturalistic to the highly stylised. Almost all the naturalistic ones located seem to come from two great carvers or carving schools. The pieces on the cover exemplify the first group, plates 11-13 the second.

About eighteen pieces of the first group have been located, six of which have a figure holding a drum. Stylistically they are so similar that they must have been carved by one school of carvers or perhaps even one carver. Their origin is Suau Island (also called South Cape). Two of the drummer pieces have a Suau provenance (MM +5919 and BMS 8335, Black Collection). The carver of at least some of these pieces is Mutuaga. This name appears on an inventory, held in the Australian Museum, of the P. G. Black collection. Under 'Suau carvings by Mutuaga' it lists massive lime knives with human figure and 'pig' handles. Presumably the spatula with a drummer figure mentioned above (BMS 8335) is one of these. Some of the spatulas of this group have betel/saliva stained blades, which shows that they were used as lime spatulas.

The present group of carvings illustrates one of the difficulties of establishing the place of manufacture for Massim spatulas. Well carved Massim pieces are often designated 'Trobriands' if no provenance is available. This is partly because the latter term is better known than the former and partly because of the belief that most well carved figurative pieces and spatulas come from the Trobriands. Hence, many published pieces of the present group are said to be from the Trobriands though there is no evidence for their having been collected there.

12. Spatula with a small human figure standing in front of a larger squatting figure (type 10). Wood. Length 250 mm (9⅞ inches). (QM E10754, ex G. F. Marks Collection 1890-1918. Photograph: QM.)

13. Spatula with a squatting human figure holding a baby (type 11). Wood. (Mme Marc de Monbrison Collection. Photograph: Mme Marc de Monbrison.)

14. Spatula with two addorsed human figures (type 12). The figures squat in a canoe. Ebony, betel-stained. Length 190 mm (7½ inches). Collected before 1901. (Author's collection. Photograph: Radomir Joura.)

The second group of stylistically distinctive naturalistic spatulas is more delicately carved and less decorated. In addition to the three pieces illustrated here, there is a spatula with a drummer figure in the Wurtzburger Collection in the Baltimore Museum of Art and there are four spatulas with squatting figures in Aberdeen and in the Glasgow Art Gallery and Museum. None of the pieces has a sound provenance.

Among stylised figurative spatulas a number of individual carving styles can be distinguished, each style presumably being the work of one carver or school of carvers and most likely of a different local-

15. Spatula with a human figure squatting in profile on top of another (type 13). Wood. Length 384 mm (15⅛ inches). (MVL Mel3556, acquired 1930. Photograph: MVL.)

16. Spatula with human figure, squatting in a relaxed position with its arms around its knees. Ebony. Length 206 mm (8⅛ inches), part of the blade missing. (AIM. Drawing: Betty Brooks.)

17. Spatula with human figure, tongue extended to chest. Shell discs tied to ears and neck. Ebony, betel-stained. Length 249 mm (9⅞ inches). Probably collected by the Reverend A. J. Viner, who lived from 1858 to 1922. (LM 1951.19.70. Photograph: LM.)

ity. The spatula in plate 6 exemplifies one individual style. Distinctive features include the particular decoration of the limbs and the unusual way the chin is carved. Several specimens in this style were collected in the Trobriands early in the twentieth century and they were presumably made there (see, for example, Shack, 1985, items 44, 45; Vargyas, 1980, photographs 4, 6). The spatula in plate 17 and the mortar in plate 75 exemplify another highly distinctive style. About seven spatulas and seven mortars have been located. They are the clearest carvings of a figure with a long, protruding tongue. Most likely this group comes from the Trobriands, which is the place of

18. Spatula with clapper handle (type 14). A human figure carved in relief on both sides. Wood. Length 430 mm (17 inches). Collected in a mainland village opposite Killerton Islands. (MM +3843, acquired 1888. Photograph: MM.)

19. Spatula with clapper handle (type 14). Represents a lizard. A shell-disc handle, *gabaela*, carved in relief below the handle. Brown wood, betel-stained. Length 445 mm (17½ inches). Collected by Peter Hallinan in Ununu Village, Milne Bay. Made by Liligowei, who died before the Second World War. (Peter Hallinan Collection. Photograph: Radomir Joura.)

20. Spatula with clapper handle (type 14). Ebony, betel-stained. Length 370 mm (15⅝ inches). Collected by Peter Hallinan on Rossel Island, 1982. (Author's collection. Photograph: Radomir Joura.)

21. Spatula with clapper handle (type 14). A ridge of interlocking birds' heads carved on one side. Brown wood. Length 285 mm (11¼ inches). (Maurice Joy Collection. Photograph: Geremy Butler.)

collection of one of the mortars (MEB 127646) and one of the spatulas (AMS E63547) carved in this style.

Almost all Massim anthropomorphic carvings have T-shaped faces, but the naturalistic figure spatulas just mentioned and some fine old spatulas with stylised figures have V-shaped faces (for example, plate 8). The spatula in plate 8 is also among the few spatulas whose figures have their sex clearly indicated.

The Trobriands were a main manufacturing centre for anthropomorphic spatulas. The Brown and Fellows Collections contain many such spatulas collected there. Jüptner (1969) shows that in his time in the Trobriands (1959-65) such spatulas were still made there. In the 1970s and 1980s at least one carver on Kitava continued to make highly stylised anthropomorphic spatulas for the tourist trade. Anthropomorphic spatulas were also made in the Marshall Bennetts and on Suau. Many other places, including Woodlark, appear as collection points for such spatulas, but there is no evidence that they were made there in any quantity.

Animal motifs

Specimens of two of the animal motif types occur in high numbers: types 14 (clappers) and 15 (snake facing into open jaws). Clappers (plates 18-21) are placed in the animal category of spatulas because they are said to represent a lizard (South Australian Museum, display case note, 1986, Narubutau, Hallinan). The tip of the handle usually has a face engraved on both sides (plate 19) and the sides of the tip sometimes have tooth-like engravings. Rossel Island clappers lack the engraved face (plate 20). Perhaps they do not represent lizards. There is no guarantee that a given design has the same meaning throughout the Massim area.

The handles of clappers are cut into two sections and hollowed

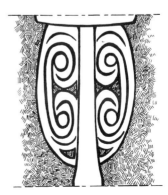

22. Design of brackets, carved below the handle of spatulas, probably unique to the Trobriands.

out to form a sound box (plate 21). In the Trobriands they are called *takakupwana* (Malinowski, not dated, Narubutau). *Kakupwana* means 'to make a clapping sound' (Koubuli). In the Trobriands properly carved clappers are reserved for chiefs. There no one may stand higher than a chief. Chiefs walking along a bushtrack use clappers to warn others of their approach (Narubutau). On Goodenough they are used to accompany dancing (Jenness and Ballantyne, 1920, page 165) and on Rossel Island to accompany singing. In the latter place they are called *dada* in imitation of the sound they make when used thus (Kaletan Wanga). About fifteen per cent of the type, including some very fine ones, are not cut through and, therefore, cannot be used as clappers.

It has already been noted that magic is a pervasive part of Massim life and that spatulas are used in magic. The clapper in plate 19 was made by Liligowei, a sorcerer who used this spatula to kill people with magic (Hallinan). Lemeki of Ebora Village, Misima, confirms that spatulas are used in magic. He says that people can be made sick or killed by being induced to use a lime stick into which certain substances have been rubbed while spells are said over it.

Clappers show that some types of spatula have been made in the Massim area by generations of carvers in a number of locations. Clappers have been collected throughout the Massim area but the place of manufacture is usually not recorded. There is so much variation in their design that it seems likely they were made in quantity in several places. The distinctive Rossel Island clappers (plate 20 and Seligman, 1916) are still made there. The Brown Collection has a few clappers collected in the Trobriands which have the brackets shown in plate 22. These brackets appear to be unique to the Trobriands. The clapper in plate 19 was made in the Milne Bay area and another fine old clapper in the Hallinan Collection (H431) was made at East Cape. The collection dates of clappers range from 1849 (MM 51.1-3.103) to 1987 (author's collection).

Spatulas of type 15 occur in great numbers (plates 23-30). Their common features are that they are slim and have a snake running down the front and the back of the handle. The front and back of the blade turns into open jaws, which appear to be swallowing the handle (or the snakes carved on it). However, seen from the side, it is the spatula's handle that turns into open jaws and seems to be swallowing the blade. Some of the spatulas of the present type have shell discs and tassels attached to them (plate 23), which magnify their value. Spatulas of type 15 are subdivided according to their different finials. The simplest version just comes to a point at the top (plate 24). Other versions have a band at the top (plate 25), a band topped with a bird (plate 26), an anthropomorphic head, a *bulabula* flower (compare type 23), an asymmetrical motif (plate 27), one squatting figure or two addorsed squatting figures (plate 28). Type 15d (plate 27) is a slightly dubious classification. The specimens located do not have the double open jaws characteristic of type 15. Narubutau remarks that the asymmetrical finial of the piece in plate 27 is reminiscent of spatulas of type 27.

The most important of the subtypes appears to be 15f. Properly carved, these spatulas are called *kenayapu* in the Trobriands and reserved for chiefs (Narubutau). The spatula in plate 28 is properly carved and has been in the sub-clan to which it belongs for about six generations (Kasaipwalova). One of its most recent owners was not a chief and therefore not permitted to use it in public. He had a much shorter copy of it made which he could use in the presence of others (plate 29). Narubutau was at first inclined to consider the piece in plate 30 a *kenayapu* but on second thoughts declared it an imitation. He said the snake's head was carved much too low on the blade, which gave it poor balance and lack of strength.

These remarks show that expert knowledge of the design and history of spatulas is required to discriminate between seemingly similar pieces. A fairly accurate copy of a *kenayapu,* not made by a master carver, does not have the power of the original. On the other hand, a poorly carved copy may have the original's power, if it is properly transferred. H433 in the Hallinan Collection is a spatula with a crudely carved anthropomorphic handle from the Daga people on the mainland, collected in the early 1980s. Although it is only a copy of the original, which broke in the early 1900s, it has the original's power to increase the fishing catch and garden yield.

The Trobriands are a main manufacturing centre for spatulas of type 15. The longest spatulas in existence are of this type and at least some of these come from Gawa. Kasaipwalova attributes the long spatula in plate 28 to Gawa on stylistic grounds. Two other informants have told the author that the vertical lines carved on the lower half of Gawa *kula* canoe splashboards represent the long spatulas made there. Specimens of type 15 have also been collected on Woodlark and in the D'Entrecasteaux, but it is unclear whether they were made there. According to Narubutau long spatulas of type 15 can be used as daggers to kill people. Tradition has it that the piece in plate 28 has been so used.

Type 16, distinguished by the circular motif on the handle, illustrates the difficulty of establishing the manufacturing centre of a design type due to the trade in spatulas. The three finest and oldest specimens located were collected in the D'Entrecasteaux in the 1930s (plate 31;

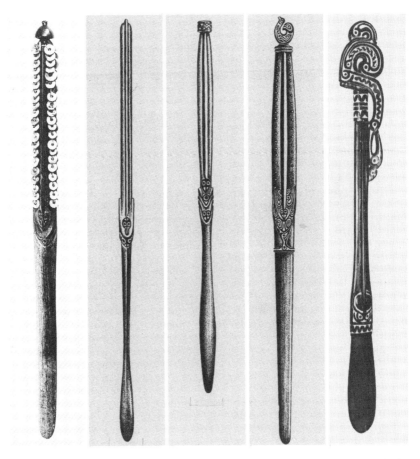

23. Spatula with a snake on the handle (type 15). Wood and shell discs, betel-stained. Length 390 mm (15⅜ inches). Collected by Sir William Macgregor on Kiriwina, 1888-98. (AUAM 246. Photograph: AUAM.)

24. Spatula with a snake on the handle; the top of the handle comes to a point (type 15a). Ebony. Length approximately 600 mm (23⅝ inches). (Henry and Luise Krips Collection. Drawing: Keith Fyfe.)

25. Spatula with a snake on the handle; the handle topped with a band of zigzags (type 15b). Ebony, betel-stained. Length 430 mm (17 inches). (Author's collection. Drawing: Keith Fyfe.)

26. Spatula with a snake on the handle; the handle topped with a bird (type 15c). Ebony. Length 700 mm (27½ inches). (Author's collection. Drawing: Keith Fyfe.)

27. Spatula with a snake on the handle; the handle topped with an asymmetrical design (type 15d). Ebony. Length 386 mm (15¼ inches). Collected by Karoly Verebelyi in the Trobriands, 1910-20. (MEB 51, 1, 6. Photograph: MEB.)

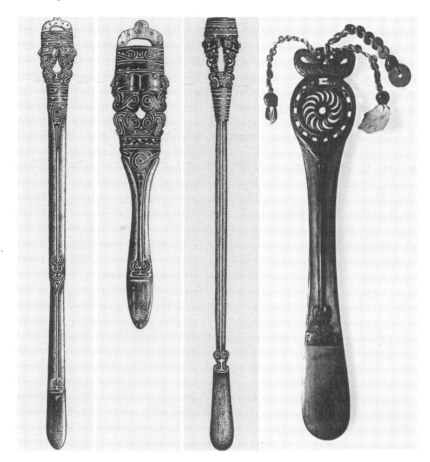

28. Spatula with a snake on the handle; the handle topped with two addorsed human figures (type 15f). *Kenayapu* type reserved for use by persons of chiefly rank. Ebony. Length approximately 700 mm (27½ inches). Held in Massim area; carved about six generations before 1983, probably on Gawa. (Drawing: Keith Fyfe.)

29. Spatula with a snake on the handle; the handle topped with two addorsed human figures (type 15). Carved in imitation of the spatula in plate 28. Ebony, betel-stained. Length approximately 300 mm (11⅞ inches). Held in Massim area; carved in the Trobriands, approximately 1970. (Drawing: Keith Fyfe.)

30. Spatula with a snake on the handle; the handle topped with two addorsed human figures (type 15). Ebony. Length 400 mm (15¾ inches). (Leo Fleischmann Collection. Drawing: Keith Fyfe.)

31. Spatula with *dana* motif (type 16). Brown wood and shell-disc tassels. Length 310 mm (12¼ inches). Collected by the Reverend John Dixon, stationed on Dobu 1923-6 and on Fergusson 1929-41. (Author's collection. Photograph: Radomir Joura.)

32. Spatula with fish and bird motif (type 17). Brown wood. Length 310 mm (12¼ inches). (MM 1944 Oc.2. 1903, ex Beasley Collection. Photograph: MM.)

Beran, 1980, illustration 3; Vargyas, 1980, photograph 47). However, another specimen, collected by E. Schlesier on Normanby in 1961-2, had been imported from the Trobriands according to the vendor (Vargyas, 1980, photograph 49). Further evidence for Trobriand manufacture of the type comes from Gerrits, who collected a specimen there in the late 1960s made by Todidayu of Okaikoda Village (Gerrits Collection number 3268). In 1987 the author interviewed this carver in Kiriwina. Todidayu said that he had invented spatulas with this design before the war (Second World War) and that the design represents a sea animal called *dana* which can be found on the beach in North Kiriwina. He said the *dana* design was just decoration and that he carved it because people think *dana* pretty. Todidayu does not know his exact age but the people in his village said that he was probably in his thirties during the war. The villagers did not know the English word for *dana* but drawings made during the interview suggest the animal is a sea-urchin. Kasaipwalova also interprets the motif under discussion as *dana*, which he translates as 'sea-urchin'.

The motif is one which the author has seen engraved on

33. Spatula, the handle carved as an unidentified animal (type 18). Wood, betel-stained. Length 563 mm (22⅛ inches). (PRM c.15.A, ex Beasley Collection and Charles Home Collection. Photograph: PRM.)

34. Spatula, the handle carved as a bird with a long curving beak (type 19). Wood, trade beads tassel, betel-stained. Length 275 mm (10⅞ inches). Collected in 1870s. (PRM C.41.A, ex Haldane Collection. Photograph: PRM.)

35. Spatula, the handle carved as a praying mantis (type 20). Brown wood. Length 343 mm (13½ inches). Collected at South Cape. (MM +3848, acquired 1888. Photograph: MM.)

36. Spatula, the handle carved as a creature with a long snout and long ears (type 21). The back of the creature carved as one side of a clapper. Brown wood. Length approximately 230 mm (9⅛ inches). Collected near Port Moresby by Waite Expedition, 1918. (SAM A10431. Photograph: SAM.)

splashboards made on Rossel Island and in the Amphletts, on the hull of a small canoe on Goodenough and, most importantly, engraved on a spatula collected before 1914 (AMS E22928). Jenness and Ballantyne also report seeing the motif on Goodenough (1920, page 199). Todidayu, therefore, cannot be the originator of the motif itself. However, all the information available is consistent with him being the first to carve this design, as the main openwork motif, on spatula handles. After the Second World War the type was also made on Kitava and Iwa. It is possible that these works are imitations of Todidayu's spatulas. If Todidayu did invent this type of spatula, then the above provides an account of the creation and spread of a spatula design.

The handle of type 17 is formed by a bird at the front of an animal head with gaping jaws (plate 32). The jaws usually show a tongue and sometimes appear carved with teeth. The open-jawed-head motif is ancient. It is engraved on a prehistoric *conus* shell found in the Trobriands around 1970 and now in the *kula* as a *mwali* (Leach and Leach, 1983, page 12).

The double motif is perhaps the most common on Massim artefacts. It occurs on the tips of northern and southern Massim *kula* canoes (called *masawa* and *nagega* respectively). On *masawa* canoes it forms the very tip of the canoe. On *nagega* canoes the bird's head in the motif in plate 50 forms the tip of the canoe and the double motif occurs immediately behind it. The double motif also occurs on Milne Bay canoe prow boards, on northern Massim dance paddles and on southern Massim canoe paddles, clubs, house and platform boards, ceremonial axe-handles and fishing-net floats. Haddon (1894, plate XII) provides a whole page of examples of the motif on various types of object.

Haddon speculated that the animal with the gaping jaws is a crocodile and the bird in front of it a frigate bird, but also mentioned that he had no field evidence for this interpretation (1894, pages 197, 210). B. A. L. Cranstone gave Haddon's speculation about the representation of frigate birds his imprimatur in *Melanesia: A Short Ethnography* (page 44). By now the belief that some birds' heads with hooked beaks carved on Massim artefacts represent frigate birds is virtually received wisdom. However, there still appears to be no field evidence for the crocodile or the frigate bird interpretation. Cecil Abel (1974) interprets the double motif as a 'barracuda which devours a frigate bird'. In conversation he adds that his Milne Bay informants told him the open-jawed animal was a fish but not which species: the barracuda interpretation is his. The author has obtained a number of interpretations of the double motif from the Massim. Walipogi Gaho of Maiwara Village in Milne Bay, a carver of canoe prow boards, states that the fish is a *gouwewe* (long-tom) and the bird a *boi* (heron). Daebo Kelesia, of Suau Village, Suau Island, states that the open-jawed head on a fishing-net float carved by him represents a fish called *odohi* and the bird with a hooked beak on another float represents a *boi*. As already mentioned, *nagega* and *masawa* canoes have a bird with a hooked beak carved at both ends. This is clearly reflected in the representation of these canoes on the spatula in plate 48 and the mortar in plate 78. Informants on Yanaba Island state that, on *nagega* canoes made there, the bird represents a *babun*. A girl bystander had a pet *babun* on a string; the bird was a pigeon. Frigate birds, called *dauta* in the local language, were hovering overhead at the time. The informants said that *dauta* were not represented on any of their carvings. Informants in Labai Village, Kiriwina, state, with respect to a *masawa* canoe keel stored there, that the motif at the tip of the canoe is a *nipawa* (grasshopper) and the open-jawed head behind it the head of a *pusa* (mullet).

The most frequent provenance for type 17 is Milne Bay villages and no doubt they were the main centre of manufacture. Their manufacture seems to have been confined to the southern part of the Massim area. Few appear to have reached the northern islands. There are none in the Brown, Fellows, Malinowski and Verebelyi Collections, made mainly or exclusively in the north. Specimens of type 17 (and those of type 26) are the least rare of those made mainly or only in the south.

The animal depicted on spatulas of type 18 (plate 33) has been speculatively interpreted as a dog, pig, crocodile and cuscus. Cecil Abel suggests that it may be a marsupial (possibly a bandicoot) about 1 foot (30 cm) long and with a long head, called *sibini*, which is common in Milne Bay. There is in the Museum of Mankind a spatula (+1586) with an animal that has a baby clinging to its belly and which could be a more naturalistic portrayal of the animal in plate 33. Another spatula in the same museum (+3406), though somewhat different again, also fits Abel's description of a *sibini*. Though usually attributed to the Trobriands, spatulas of type 18 are made on Suau. Two of the fourteen specimens located were collected there (MM +3847 and BMS, Black Collection, number C8337). The collection place of the others is unknown. Stylistically the animal carvings of type 18 are identical to the naturalistic anthropomorphic carvings shown on the cover of this book. Both must be the work of the same carver or school of carvers on Suau. As already noted above, an inventory of the P. G. Black Collection names Mutuaga as the carver (or one of the carvers) responsible. The spatula in plate 33 has a betel/saliva deposit on its blade, which shows that at least some

37. Spatula with thirteen birds and a snake carved on the handle (type 22). Wood. Length 413 mm (16¼ inches). (Glasgow Art Gallery and Museum 99-61 n, acquired 1899. Photograph: Glasgow Art Gallery and Museum.)

38. Spatula, the handle carved as an unidentified creature. Wood, betel-stained. Length approximately 220 mm (8⅝ inches). (MM 87.2-7.221, ex H. H. Romilly Collection, collected before 1887. Photograph: MM.)

39. Spatula, the handle carved as a standing bird. Wood and trade beads. Length 210 mm (8¼ inches). (AMS E70227. Photograph: Ric Bolzan.)

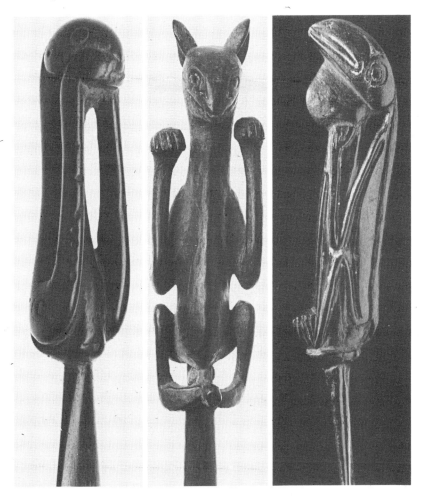

40. Spatula, the handle carved as an unidentified animal. Ebony. Length 205 mm (8⅛ inches). (MM +1591, acquired 1882. Photograph: MM.)

41. Spatula, the handle carved as a tree kangaroo. Brown wood, betel-stained. Length 381 mm (15 inches). (MM +3409, acquired 1886. Photograph: MM.)

42. Spatula, the handle carved as a (?) lizard. Wood. (UMC Z10078. Photograph: UMC.)

43. (Far left) Spatula with *bulabula* flower motif (type 23). Wood. Length 288 mm (11⅜ inches). (QM El087, ex G. F. Marks Collection, 1890-1918. Photograph: QM.)

44. (Left) Spatula with disc-shaped handle representing a (?) wild yam (type 24). Ebony. Length 265 mm (10½ inches). (AMS E22928, collected before 1915. Photograph: Ric Bolzan.)

45. (Above) Morning-star motif, engraved on some spatulas with disc-shaped handles (type 24).

specimens of the type were used by the Massim themselves.

Type 19 has a bird with a stylised body and a long curving beak as a handle (plate 34). None of the pieces located has a recorded place of collection, but they are likely to have a southern Massim origin.

Type 20 obviously represents a praying mantis. The piece in plate 35 was collected on South Cape. Other specimens are in the Royal Museum of Scotland, Edinburgh, and, as Haddon noted (1894, page 210), in the Ethnographical Museum, Dresden. One of the two Dresden pieces was collected in the D'Entrecasteaux.

The handle of type 21 is a creature with a long snout and long ears. This creature, perhaps an animal or mythical being, seems to be connected with black magic. The piece illustrated in plate 36, though collected near Port Moresby, is certainly of Massim origin. An identical piece, in the author's collection, was obtained at the magistrate's court in Samarai in 1932. It comes from two Buhutu Valley men who had taken it from their grandmother, a notorious sorcerer, after killing her. Further evidence for the connection of the figure with magic comes from Abel (1974), who reports seeing a carved wooden 'spirit figure about 4 feet (1.3 metres) high with a long snout and huge ears' in a Milne Bay village. In conversation he adds that this figure had come to the coast from the Buhutu Valley where it had been used by a sorcerer. A third spatula of the type, by a different hand from the other two, is in the National Museum, Wellington.

Type 22 has a handle with two rows of birds (plate 37). Of the ten specimens located, half were collected in the Trobriands.

Plates 38-42 illustrate some exceptionally fine unique zoomorphic spatulas.

Plant motifs

Type 23 (plate 43) is called *tabulabula* in the Trobriands (Malinowski, not dated, Narubutau). It represents the *bulabula* flower. The type is made in the Trobriands. Vakutans recognise it as a master carver design, but anyone can use such spatulas. Some specimens have been collected on Iwa and the type is almost certainly also made there.

Type 24 is distinguished by its disc-shaped handle. Some of these round handles are beautifully scrolled (plate 44); others carry the motif in plate 45. In the Trobriands this type represents two quite different things, a wild yam (because of its shape?) and the morning star (if it carries the star-shaped engraving). In virtue of the former representation it is called *taubwara* (Campbell, personal communication, 1987), in virtue of the latter *takubwana* (Malinowski, reported in Shack, 1985, pages 54-5). The morning-star motif is also found on painted Trobriand warshields and southern Massim canoe splashboards. Campbell notes that there was disagreement among her Vakutan informants as to whether *taubwara* is a master carver design and disagreement between her Vakutan and her Kiriwinan informants as to what this type of spatula represents and what it is called. According to Shack (1985, page 55), Malinowski reports that the type represents a fruit. It is clear that this type is carved in the Trobriands. Campbell's informants recognised it as a local design and there are several specimens in the Brown, Fellows, Malinowski and Verebelyi Collections, made in the Trobriands.

The names for spatulas of type 24 are formed from the word *tai* (to carve) and the word for the thing represented, *ubwara* (wild yam) and *kubwana* (morning star). This appears to be a typical way to form names of types of spatula in Kiriwinan.

Artefact motifs

Types 25 (plates 46-8), 26 (plates 49, 51, 52), 27 (plate 53) and 28 (plate 54) represent canoes, parts of canoes or steering paddles. Since the Massim are seafaring people, this symbolism is hardly surprising. The handle of the spatula in plate 46 shows an animal riding

46. Spatula, the handle carved as a highly stylised canoe with an animal rider (type 25). Wood. Length approximately 300 mm (11⅞ inches). (AMS E33105, acquired 1930. Photograph: Ric Bolzan.)

47. Spatula, the handle carved as a canoe prow or stern board, *tabuya,* resting on a canoe carved disproportionately small (type 25). Wood, betel-stained. Length 273 mm (10¾ inches). Collected by the Reverend S. B. Fellows in the Trobriands 1891-1901. (ANG. Photograph: Arthur Nutt.)

48. Spatula with canoe-shaped handle, probably representing a *nagega* canoe (type 25). Wood. Length approximately 330 mm (13 inches). (SAM A9075, collected before 1914. Drawing: Keith Fyfe.)

49. Spatula with a canoe-tip design handle (type 26). Ebony. Length 265 mm (10½ inches). Made by Kaletan Wanga, Demjo Village, Rossel Island, 1986. Collected there by the author, 1987. (Author's collection. Photograph: Radomir Joura.)

in a stylised canoe. The Massim often take pigs on *kula* trips. It is pointless, however, to speculate about the nature of the animal rider. In a culture in which *boi* (herons) are carved with straight or curved beaks and fish with long tongues, in which representational carving ranges from the accurate to the totally stylised and in which there are mythical beings, only field evidence can establish the nature of this animal rider. The spatula in plate 47 represents a *tabuya* (carved board at prow and stern of the canoe) sitting on a *masawa* canoe hull. The spatula in plate 48 shows a particularly fine three-dimensional carving of a canoe. It seems most likely that the spatulas representing *masawa* canoes are made by the people who make these canoes, that is, those of the Trobriands, of Iwa or of the D'Entrecasteaux. The piece in plate 47 was probably collected in the Trobriands. Some of the other spatulas with more or less complete canoe handles also have a northern Massim feel. The piece in plate 48 is reminiscent of a *nagega* canoe in shape and so perhaps was carved in one of the many places where these canoes are or were made. Since the piece is old, this includes the Trobriands, where *nagega* canoes were made up to the nineteenth century. The Rattlesnake collected a canoe-shaped spatula on Brumer Island in the extreme south of the Massim area (MM 51.1-3.104). Most likely canoe-shaped spatulas are made in the north and south.

The spatula in plate 49 justifies the grouping together of about sixty spatulas as type 26. It was purchased in 1987, in Demjo Village, Rossel Island, from Kaletan Wanga, who had made it. He said that the spatula is called *kokonu (koko* = canoe, *nu* = tip) because it represents a canoe tip. Leonard Veveloga, a bystander, added that *koko* was not the local word for canoe, but that used in Tagula. Kaletan Wanga had seen Peter, of Ule Island in the Rossel Group, carve spatulas of this design and then he carved them too. Informants in Ulugwa Village, Ule Island, confirmed that Peter Uya, who died about 1960, was a well known carver of spatulas.

The most prominent motif on spatulas of type 26 is that shown in plate 50. The same motif is carved on *nagega* canoe tips. The

50. Bird motif carved on the tips of *nagega* canoes and the handles of spatulas of type 26.

51. Spatula with a canoe-tip design handle (type 26). Ebony, betel-stained, surface engraving unfinished. Length 270 mm (10⅝ inches). (MM +1592, acquired 1882. Photograph: MM.)

52. Spatula with a canoe-tip design handle (type 26). Ebony. Length 285 mm (11¼ inches). (Author's collection. Photograph: Radomir Joura.)

53. Spatula with handle which represents a *nagega* canoe motif (type 27). Ebony. Length 255 mm (10 inches). (Leo Fleischmann Collection. Photograph: Radomir Joura.)

54. Spatula which represents a canoe steering oar (type 28). Ebony, betel-stained. Length 255 mm (10 inches). Collected by P. Baron de Rautenfeld, 1920s. (Museum für Völkerkunde, Basle, Vb 14093. Photograph: Museum für Völkerkunde, Basle.)

55. (Top left) Spatula carved in imitation of a shell-disc handle, *gabaela* (type 29). Wood, betel-stained. Length 230 mm (9 inches). Collected by Owen Stanley Expedition in the Louisiades, 1849. (MM 51.1-3.161. Photograph: MM.)

56. (Bottom) Spatula and shell-disc handle (type 29). Turtleshell and shell discs. Length 283 mm (11⅛ inches). (QM E8456, acquired before 1900. Photograph: QM.)

57. (Top right) Shell-disc handle, *gabaela*. Wood, shell discs and mother-of-pearl shell sections. Length 430 mm (17 inches). Collected by Jutta and Sergei Malnic on Paneati, 1983. (Jutta and Sergei Malnic Collection. Photograph: Harry Beran.)

spatulas in plates 51 and 52 also carry this motif and can, therefore, be regarded as representing *nagega* canoe tips, although they differ in other features. The three specimens of type 26 illustrated show how much scope for variety of design there is within a basic motif. The great variation in design suggests that this type is also made in southern locations other than Rossel Island. Recorded collection places include South Cape, Teste Island and Woodlark. There are no specimens in the Trobriand collections made by Brown, Fellows, Malinowski and Verebelyi. Type 26 is one of the two least rare types peculiar to the south.

Type 27 (plate 53) may be a variation of the canoe-tip design and, therefore, not a distinct type. Specimens of the type are extremely uniform in design, that illustrated being typical. There are seven specimens in the Brown Collection, all but one collected in the Trobriands. Firth (1979, page 56) illustrates three specimens, collected on Vakuta. He reports that one of them 'is said to represent *Nagega,* a Murua (that is, Woodlark) canoe'. Campbell's Vakutan informants told her that the type is recognised there as a master carver design called *tanagega.* It is clear that this type was made on Vakuta and perhaps it was made only there. The carving of this design there dates back to the nineteenth century when *nagega* canoes were still made in the Trobriands.

Type 28 (plate 54) represents a steering paddle. These paddles are large and heavy and have a looped grip at the top (see Beran, 1980, illustration 73). Strength and endurance are needed to use the oar. Not only is the canoe steered with it but, because either end of the canoe can point ahead, the steerer often has to carry the oar from one end of the canoe to the other. Malinowski, not dated, writes that some spatulas represent a 'steering rudder' and are called *takuriga* in the Trobriands. (*Kuriga* is the Kiriwinan word for steering.) None of the spatulas in his collection, however, clearly resembles a steering oar, including that published by Shack as a specimen (1985, illustration 35). However, Narubutau interprets the top of the spatula in plate 54 as a *tolawaya,* that is, the top of a steering oar, thus confirming Malinowski's information. Kasaipwalova adds that *tolawaya* is associated with the idea of tenacity: both hands are necessary when one is using a steering oar. Only two other examples have been located. One of these (MM 1950 Oc.2.10) was collected in the Trobriands.

Type 29 (plates 55, 56) seems to be an imitation of the wooden crescent-topped handle for shell discs (plate 57) traded throughout the Louisiades and called *gabaela* in some parts of this archipelago. *Gabaela* are perforated along the top of the crescent for the attach-

58. (Right) Spatula, imitation of bone spatula of type 40 (type 30). Turtleshell with shell disc and banana seed attachment. Length 240 mm (9½ inches). (MM 9162. Photograph: MM.)

59. (Far right) Spatula, imitation of bone spatula of type 40 (type 30). Brown wood. Length 330 mm (13 inches). (Author's collection, ex Pitt-Rivers Collection, Dorset, and W. B. Webster, 1898. Photograph: Radomir Joura.)

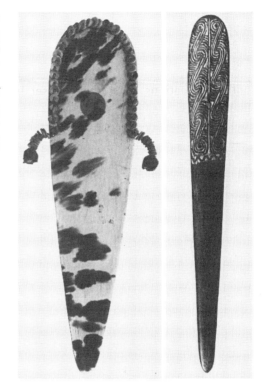

ment of shell discs. It is the shell discs which make the object valuable, not the handle. The object is used to pay for feasts, land, canoes and other things. Old, well carved *gabaela* are usually uniform in size and design, that illustrated in plate 57 being typical in both respects. Two stylised birds' heads are always carved below the crescent on both sides of the object. *Gabaela* are not normally used as lime spatulas. The wooden spatula imitations of *gabaela* are much smaller than *gabaela,* they have no or few holes for shell discs and they often depart considerably from the design typical of *gabaela. Gabaela* are made on Tagula and perhaps only there. The wooden spatula imitations of them are probably made in the south and the north of the Massim area. The spatula illustrated in plate 55 was collected in the Louisiades and is an unusually accurate copy of a *gabaela.* The Brown and Fellows Collections each contain one wooden spatula of type 29, collected in the Trobriands. Their shape suggests that they are imitations of *gabaela* made by Trobrianders who had seen *gabaela*

60. Spatula with loop-shaped handle (type 31). Ebony, betel-stained. Length 266 mm (10½ inches). Collected by Geza Roheim on Normanby, 1930. (MEB 131568. Photograph: MEB.)

61. Spatula, the handle loop shaped with an internal rib (type 32). Wood, betel-stained. Length 330 mm (13 inches). Collected by Sir William Macgregor. (QM M937, acquired 1892. Photograph: QM.)

62. Spatula with ring-shaped handle (type 33). Brown wood. (Sir David Attenborough Collection. Photograph: Sir David Attenborough.)

63. Spatula, the handle shaped as a ring with internal projection (type 34). Wood, betel-stained. Length approximately 310 mm (12¼ inches). (MM +1710, acquired 1882. Photograph: MM.)

64. (Right) Spatula, the handle carved as a bar, square in cross-section (type 35). Wood, betel-stained. Collected by the Reverend George Brown in the Trobriands, 1890-1905. (NMEO 26.79.86. Photograph: Hancock Museum, Newcastle.)

65. (Centre right) Spatula with flat, oblong handle (type 36). Length approximately 350 mm (13⅞ inches). (MM +6348, acquired 1893. Photograph: MM.)

66. (Far right) Spatula with long flat handle rounded at the top (type 37). Wood. Length 315 mm (12⅜ inches). (AMS E72408. Photograph: Ric Bolzan.)

but had only a limited desire or ability to imitate them accurately.

The suggestion that wooden spatulas of type 29 are imitations of *gabaela,* if correct, would explain their rather awkward shape. The suggestion is perhaps also supported by the betel-nut pestle in plate 87, which appears to be carved in the shape of a *gabaela,* and the representation of a *gabaela,* in relief, on the clapper in plate 19. Maria Lepowsky (Leach and Leach, 1983, page 485), however, refers to *gabaela* as oversized ceremonial lime sticks. This suggests that *gabaela* developed out of crescent-shaped lime sticks instead of the lime sticks being imitations of the *gabaela.* Giant versions of some spatula types are indeed made, possibly for ceremonial purposes. For example, the Cambridge University Museum of Anthropology

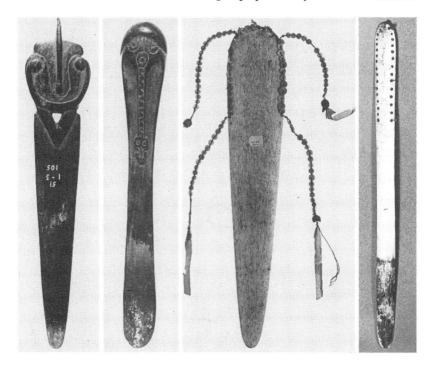

67. Spatula, oval handle with a bar pointing into a crescent (type 38). Wood, betel-stained. Length 185 mm (7¼ inches). Collected by Owen Stanley Expedition in the Louisiades, 1849. (MM 51.1-3.105. Photograph: MM.)

68. Spatula, the handle rounded at the top and showing a snake carved in relief (type 39). Wood, betel-stained. Length 180 mm (7⅛ inches). Collected by Cooke Daniels Expedition, 1904. (MM 1906.10-13.1400. Photograph: MM.)

69. Spatula with rounded top tapering towards the tip (type 40). Whalebone with shell-disc, wild banana seed and leaf decoration. Length 400 mm (15¾ inches). (MM 87.2-7.236, acquired 1886. Photograph: MM.)

70. Spatula of straight shape with rounded top (type 42). Human bone, pierced for the attachment of shell discs, betel-stained. Length 229 mm (9 inches). Collected by the Reverend S. B. Fellows in the Trobriands, 1891-1901. (ANG. Photograph: Arthur Nutt.)

has a clapper and a *tanagega* spatula which, at 60 cm (24 inches), are twice the normal length of these types of spatula and not easy to use for their normal purpose. Only further fieldwork can determine whether the wooden lime spatulas of type 29 are indeed imitations of *gabaela* or *gabaela* ceremonial versions of the spatulas.

The artefact in plate 56 serves a double function. As the full complement of shell discs shows, objects of this type are true shell-disc handles. As such, like *gabaela,* they serve as 'tribal currency'. But, unlike *gabaela,* they are often also used as lime spatulas, even when fully supplied with shell discs. Their smaller size and weight facilitate this. They circulate throughout the Louisiades. According to Lepowsky they are made only on Tagula (page 485), but Wanim informants say that they also make them. The classification of the turtleshell handles for shell discs *cum* lime spatulas as imitations of the *gabaela* is largely speculative.

The turtleshell and wooden versions of type 30 (plates 58, 59) are imitations, in a more readily available material, of the rare type 40 (plate 69). The latter are made of bone, carry shell discs and are restricted to leading men. The wooden imitations usually lack the shell discs; the turtleshell ones usually carry them. Of the few specimens located, few have known collection places. Southern Massim origin seems most likely since this is the origin of type 40.

Non-representational motifs and abstract designs

It seems likely that types 31 to 39 (plates 60-8) include some spatulas the handles of which have a representational significance, but one not known outside the Massim area, and others whose handles carry non-representational designs. Type 31 (plate 60) was still made in the southernmost part of Kiriwina and in Vakuta in the early 1960s, according to Jüptner (1969). Campbell also reports that Vakutans recognise this type as a local design. The Trobriands, Woodlark and the D'Entrecasteaux are the most common collection places. Several specimens of type 35 (plate 64) were collected in the Trobriands, a few in the Marshall Bennetts, the rest throughout the Massim area. Types 36 and 37 (plates 65, 66) seem to be collected most frequently in the Trobriands, Woodlark and D'Entrecasteaux. The only specimen of type 38 with a recorded place of collection (the Louisiades) is that illustrated in plate 67. Most of the specimens of type 39 (plate 68) which have been located were collected by the Cooke Daniels Expedition. Three were collected in Kwaiawata and Iwa; the collection place of the others is lost.

Three types of spatula are carved from bone. Type 40 is carved from whale or dugong bone. The piece in plate 69 shows the shape and shell decoration typical of the type. Spatulas of this type are rare, valuable and restricted to village leaders and wealthy individuals. A good canoe can be obtained for a spatula of the size illustrated. They are *kula* items which travel in the same direction as *mwali* armbands and are exchanged for *soulava* necklaces (Narubutau, Malinowski, 1966, pages 355, 358). They are called *bosu* in the Trobriands (Narubutau) and *potuma* in Milne Bay (Seligman, 1910,

71. (Far left) Spatula with a handle hollowed out for use as a betel-nut mortar (type 43). Blackpalm. Length 385 mm (15⅛ inches). (Author's collection. Photograph: Radomir Joura.)

72. (Centre left) Spatula, the conical handle carved as a betel-nut mortar (type 44). Ebony, betel-stained. Length 180 mm (7⅛ inches). Collected by Sir William Macgregor. (QM M1204, acquired 1892. Photograph: QM.)

73. (Left) Spatula, the handle carved as a pestle for crushing betel-nuts (type 45). A *bulabula* flower motif carved between handle and blade. Wood. Collected by the Reverend R. S. Lawton in Lalela Village, Kitava, 1960s. (SAM. A58913. Photograph: SAM.)

page 515). Of the few specimens with a recorded collection place, most show southern Massim collection and this is almost certainly the place of manufacture.

Type 41 is made from cassowary bone, which is imported into the

Trobriands from the mainland. They are called *gesuwali* (Narubutau) and are a symbol of chiefly status. Plate 2 shows the chief of Lobua Village of Kiriwina with his limepot and *gesuwali*, decorated with the white cowrie shells which are also a sign of chiefly status.

Type 42 (plate 70) is made from the bones of deceased relatives in the Trobriands and the Marshall Bennetts. Malinowski (1982, pages 133-4) reports that Trobrianders have mixed feelings about the use of spatulas made from the bones of a husband or father. In the Trobriands the dead are buried twice. A day after the first burial the body is exhumed, the skull is made into a limepot and some of the bones into spatulas. The use of the relics brings back pleasant memories of the deceased, but it is also regarded 'as a harsh and unpleasant duty, as a pious repayment for all the benefits received from the father'. The bones are used for some years, passed to more distant relations and finally deposited in caves.

Non-representational double-purpose spatulas

Spatulas of types 43 (plate 71), 44 (plate 72) and 45 (plate 73) serve two functions. Types 43 and 44 are also betel-nut mortars. The former type is carved in blackpalm. The handle consists of a length of the trunk of the palm and the mortar is a hollow dug into one or both ends of the handle. None of those located has a recorded collection place. There is little evidence of blackpalm being used by Trobriand or Marshall Bennett carvers. Most likely, therefore, type 43 is made further south. Type 44 is usually carved in ebony and the mortar is fully sculpted at the end of the handle. Several have been collected in the Trobriands and this is probably the origin of most of them. Type 45 has a handle which serves as a pestle. Plate 73 shows an unusual specimen of the type since it also seems to carry the *bulabula* motif.

About twenty per cent of spatulas do not fall into recognisable types. Plates 16, 17 and 38-42 show some of the finest. Some of these may be the only specimens of traditional types which survive. Others may be 'one-offs'.

74. Betel-nut mortar and pestle in use. (Photograph: R. A. Vivian, about 1917. Photograph held in National Museum of Victoria, copyright of the Archaeological and Anthropological Society of Victoria, Melbourne.)

4
Mortars, pestles, limepots and baskets

This chapter presents a typology of the mortars and pestles which are used by people with poor teeth to crush betel-nuts, of the pots in which the lime used in betel chewing is kept and of the baskets in which all the utensils are stored or carried. Large limepots are often carried on a suspension cord rather than in a basket.

Mortars and pestles

In the Trobriands mortars are called *kaipita* and pestles *kaimili*. Plate 74 shows the utensils in use. Human, animal, plant and artefact representations occur on them, However, only a small number of traditional types of design can be identified. Mortars are carved in anthropomorphic shape (type 1), drum shape (type 2) and canoe shape (type 3). Specimens of each type are rare. Mortars are also decorated with various animal motifs (but no types have been identified) and carved in barrel shape without any identifiable representational significance.

Plate 75 shows a typical example of mortars of type 1. It is clearly the product of the same school of carvers which produced the spatula in plate 17. Another mortar of this type was collected in the Trobriands (MEB 127646). The drum handle at the back of some of the anthropomorphic mortars also points to Trobriand manufacture, since the larger Trobriand drums represent humans. Plate 76 shows an unusual mortar of complete human form. According to notes in the Museum of Ethnography, Budapest, the figure is a female with an enlarged clitoris. Several mortars exist with a more incidental representation of human figures, for example, with one figure on each side of the base of the mortar. At least some of these are made in the Trobriands.

The second type of representational mortar is drum-shaped. The finest specimen (plate 77) is uniquely carved in whalebone, clearly represents a Trobriands/Marshall Bennetts drum and was collected in the Trobriands. A few other, wooden, ones have also been collected in the Trobriands. In 1983 the author acquired one on Egum Atoll, which had been made there.

The third type of mortar is canoe-shaped. The specimen illustrated (plate 78) has the prow and stern boards of a *masawa* canoe carved only in the Trobriands, Iwa and the D'Entrecasteaux. The Trobriand archipelago is the most common recorded collection place of canoe-

75. (Right) Betel-nut mortar in human and drum shape; the figure's tongue extended to the chest. Wood. Length 180 mm (7⅛ inches). (AMS E7568. Photograph: Ric Bolzan.)

76. (Far right) Betel-nut mortar in the shape of a female figure with an enlarged clitoris. Wood. Length 270 mm (10⅝ inches). Collected by Geza Roheim on Normanby, 1930. (MEB 1311750. Photograph: MEB.)

shaped mortars, though two pieces, carved in rather different styles from that illustrated here, were collected in the Suau area (Hallinan Collection) and on Normanby (Schlesier, 1986, illustration 28). The last mentioned was made on Normanby.

Several mortars are more or less cone-shaped with an animal carving at the base of the mortar. Plate 79 shows one of these. Newton suggests the carving on it is a praying mantis (1975, illustration 22). The mortar in plate 80, obviously of very considerable age, could possibly have some relationship to the fish and bird motif of spatula type 17. However, the animal at the end of the open jaws looks more like a snake or lizard than a bird. Barrel-shaped mortars without any obvious representational features are quite common, but the engrav-

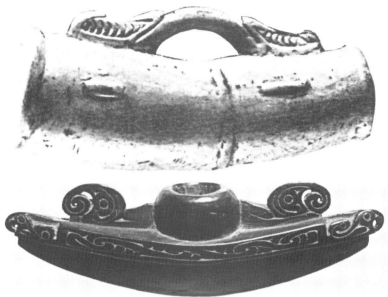

77. (Top) Betel-nut mortar in the shape of a Trobriand drum. Whalebone. Length 108 mm (4¼ inches). Collected by P. G. Black in the Trobriands, 1886-1916. (BMS 9424. Photograph: George Barrows in Newton.)

78. (Above) Betel-nut mortar in the shape of a *masawa* canoe, with prow and stern boards, *tabuya*. Ebony. Length 205 mm (8⅛ inches). Collected by Captain W. C. Thomson around 1900. (Author's collection. Photograph: Radomir Joura.)

79. (Left) Betel-nut mortar decorated with a (?) praying mantis. Ebony. Length 170 mm (6⅝ inches). Collected by Ronald Woodward on Woodlark, 1913. (Friede Collection, ex S. G. Moriarty Collection. Photograph: Radomir Joura.)

80. Betel-nut mortar decorated with an animal head with open jaws and a protruding tongue; a small animal at the front of the open jaws. Wood. Length 100 mm (3⅞ inches). Collected in the D'Entrecasteaux Islands. (MM +1703, acquired 1883. Photograph: MM.)

81. Betel-nut mortar, barrel-shaped with elaborate incised design. Brown wood. Length 137 mm (5⅜ inches). Collected by Clare Harding on Kiriwina, 1983. (Clare Harding Collection. Photograph: Radomir Joura.)

82. Betel-nut mortar decorated with a stylised bird. Wood. Length 75 mm (3 inches). Collected by Cooke Daniels Expedition on Kwaiawata, 1904. (MM 1906. 10-13.1445. Photograph: MM.)

83. Betel-nut mortar in the shape of an animal head. Wood. Length 120 mm (4¾ inches). Collected in Voborobo Village on Woodlark Island, 1889-90. (Pigorini Museum 44529. Photograph: Pigorini Museum.)

84. Betel-nut pestle with splayed human figure; bottom half recarved, probably from a broken spatula. Wood. Length 210 mm (8¼ inches). Collected by Sir William Macgregor between 1888 and 1898. (AUAM 193. Photograph: AUAM.)

85. Betel-nut pestle with human head. Ebony. Length 134 mm (5¼ inches). Collected by Captain W. C. Thomson around 1900. (Author's collection. Photograph: Radomir Joura.)

86. Betel-nut pestle with bird motif. Ebony. Length 260 mm (10¼ inches). Collected by the author on Kaileuna, 1983. (Author's collection. Photograph: Radomir Joura.)

87. Betel-nut pestle with a crescent-shaped top, probably representing a shell-disc handle, *gabaela*. Wood. Length 220 mm (8⅝ inches). (EMS 1916.1.755, Dr Robert Pulleine Collection, formed in the 1870s. Photograph: EMS.)

88. Betal-nut pestle with *bulabula* flower motif. Wood. Length 265 mm (10½ inches). Collected by Clare Harding on Kiriwina, 1983. (Clare Harding Collection. Photograph: Radomir Joura.)

ing on some appears to be more than mere decoration (plate 81).

On the pestles used with betel-nut mortars, anthropomorphic and bird motifs are most common (plates 84-6). Other motifs, such as the *gabaela* crescent (plate 87) and the *bulabula* flower (plate 88) are very rare. On the anthropomorphic pestles, usually only the head (or head and arms) of the figure is portrayed. The pestle in plate 84 is unusual in having such a splendid splayed figure as a handle but did not originate as a pestle. It was recarved from a (broken?) spatula or staff. It is included here to show that the practice of converting carvings from one kind to another, found in the Massim area, also applies to betel-chewing equipment.

Mortars and pestles are decorated less than spatulas, presumably because elaborate sculptural carving interferes with their use. At least in the Trobriands, betel-nut mortars and pestles have two secondary functions. They are used for mixing the magical concoction which apprentices have to drink to internalise master carver knowledge (Beran, 1980, page 9) and for mixing and applying facial paint (Malinowski, 1966, pages 151-2).

Limepots

In the Trobriands limepots are called *yaguma*. A number of types can be distinguished. Most are made from gourds, some from coconuts. Some are made from human skulls but none of these has been located. The pots made from gourds have a stopper made from a rolled-up leaf covered with woven fibres. Some stoppers carry a pig's tusk, which may be a twentieth-century innovation. In the Trobriands, the limepots of chiefs are embellished with shell discs, tassels and white cowrie shells. Plate 89 shows the most famous type of the Massim limepots with its characteristic all-over burnt-in decoration. They carry longer stoppers than other types but no boar's tusk. Their manufacture ceased around 1900. According to Malinowski, not dated, these pots were made in northern Kiriwina, though Webster catalogues show some as having been collected in the Louisiades (Catalogue 12, number 156 and Catalogue 15, number 78). It is possible that they got there through trade. The pot in plate 90 shows another typical nineteenth-century style of decoration, especially of small pots, which died out at the turn of the century. The absence of a tusk is again typical. Many limepots have no burnt-in decoration, including some used by chiefs (plate 2). In the twentieth century Kiriwinans started decorating pots with a band of fine scrolling around the middle (plate 91). Many such pots are sold to tourists. But fine specimens, such as that illustrated, are also used by Trobrianders.

89. Limepot made from a gourd with all-over burnt-in decoration and a stopper made from rolled-up leaf and woven fibres. Height 255 mm (10 inches). (MM 3825, acquired in 1867. Photograph: MM.)

90. Limepot made from a gourd with some burnt-in decoration and a stopper made from rolled-up leaf and woven fibres. Height 100 mm (3⅞ inches). Collected by Henry Tryon, 1895. (Author's collection. Photograph: Radomir Joura.)

91. Limepot made from a gourd with burnt-in scrolled decoration around the middle and a stopper made from rolled-up leaf, woven fibre and a pig's tusk. Height 320 mm (12⅝ inches). Collected by Anthony J. P. Meyer on Kaileuna, 1987. (Anthony J. P. Meyer Collection. Photograph: Anthony J. P. Meyer.)

92. Limepot made from a coconut with wooden stopper. Height approximately 70 mm (2¾ inches). Collected by Professor Erhard Schlesier on Normanby, 1961-2. (Georg-August University, Göttingen, Oz.3168. Photograph: Hans-Joachim Gross.)

Vanoi, the paramount chief of Kiriwina until his death in 1982, left such a pot, richly embellished with shells, shell discs and a large tusk, in his estate. Both the pots without burnt-in designs and those with a band of scrolling typically carry a boar's tusk. Limepots are also made from coconuts, often with a wooden stopper (plate 92).

On some islands, limepots have secondary uses. In the D'Entre-casteaux they are used as musical instruments: they are hit with a comb to accompany singing (Lawson, 1983) and dancing (Jenness and Ballantyne, 1920, page 165). In Ebora Village, Misima, a limepot may be beaten with a spatula while something important is publicly said, for example, while a feast is being announced (Lemeki).

Baskets

There are at least three types of basket in which betel-chewing paraphernalia are kept. Plate 93 shows an envelope-shaped basket which is carried under the arm and called *kauya* in Kiriwina. It is basic equipment for Trobrianders. Very similar baskets are used elsewhere, for example, on Egum Atoll. Plate 94 shows a set of nested baskets with a carrying strap, made in the Trobriands and called *tanepopo* there (Shack, 1985, page 82). The outer basket contains two inner ones. This enables a Trobriander of rank to hide some of his betel-nuts, which, if visible to others, he would, on the principle of *noblesse oblige,* have to distribute among them. Its threefold con-

93. Envelope-shaped basket for betel-chewing paraphernalia. Leaf material. Length 340 mm (13⅜ inches). Collected by author on Kiriwina, 1987. (Author's collection. Photograph: Radomir Joura.)

struction is also a symbol of the man's wealth (Malinowski, 1978, pages 40-1). The pliable round basket in plate 95 is made in the Louisiades and is popular there for carrying betel-chewing items. On Wanim it is called *tiltil*.

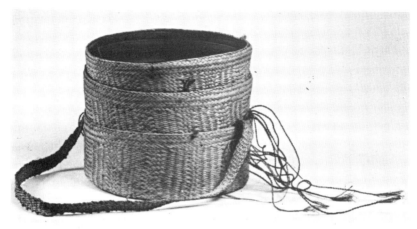

94. Nested baskets for betel-chewing paraphernalia. Plaited pandanus leaf with banana-leaf interior reinforcement and a carrying strap. Made in the Trobriands. (MEB 127568B. Photograph: MEB.)

95. Round basket for betel-chewing paraphernalia. Plaited vegetable fibres. Diameter 250 mm (9⅞ inches). Collected by the author on Wanim, 1983. (Author's collection. Photograph: Harry Beran.)

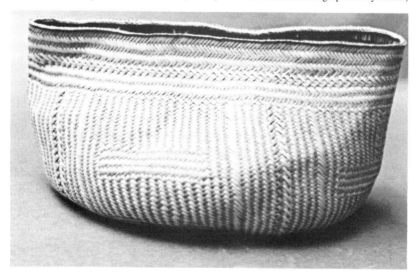

5
Concluding remarks

What is here called the 'paradigm method' has been used to identify and interpret some of the spatula types. For example, some spatulas have a vaguely canoe-shaped handle. These can be grouped together as a type because there are other spatulas whose handles represent a canoe with total clarity (the paradigms) and because it is clear that the representation of things in Massim art ranges from the near naturalistic to the highly stylised. According to Shack (1985, pages 54-5), Malinowski collected spatulas that represent cooking spoons and dance paddles. These types have not been included here because no paradigm spatulas have been located. The spatulas illustrated in Shack, as representing a cooking spoon and a dance paddle (illustrations 34 and 36), may indeed represent these objects, but they do not do so clearly enough.

A great number of types of spatula have been distinguished. During the history of the Massim, new types of spatula must have been invented and others abandoned. However, the period during which spatulas were collected, before their production declined because of the impact of the West, is too short for much evidence of such changes. As noted, design type 16 seems to be one that was invented in Kiriwina in the 1930s and which has spread to Kitava and the Marshall Bennetts.

There is also considerable scope for artistic creativity within a type of design. The spatulas in plates 49, 51 and 52, which seem to be variations on the canoe-tip theme, illustrate this. Plate 14 shows another delightful instance of originality. Normally, two addorsed figures forming a spatula handle are carved squatting on the same kind of platform found below the figures in plates 12 and 13. The carver of the spatula in plate 14, however, has turned the uninteresting platform into a miniature canoe.

The typology presented here, like most typologies, is not totally exhaustive, makes some arbitrary distinctions and oversimplifies and distorts reality to some extent. In addition to spatulas with long, flat, oblong handles (type 36) and those with long, flat handles with a rounded end (type 37), there are also a few with flat, square handles (plate 96). Perhaps these should be added as an extra type. Some of the spatulas of type 24, which represent a wild yam, also represent the morning star. So an extra category of types could be listed: natural phenomena motifs. And there is, of course, the very large mixed motif type 15, that is, spatulas with a snake facing into open jaws. This motif is common to them all, but their finials vary a great deal, showing human, bird and plant motifs. They could therefore be listed under a broad category of mixed motif spatulas. Moreover, the concept of representation has been stretched to that of mere imitation in the case of type 30.

The main centres for the manufacture of traditional types of spatula and mortar are the Trobriands, the Marshall Bennetts, Rossel Island, the Milne Bay area, Tagula and Suau Island. Clearly, these items were also made elsewhere in smaller numbers and this is reflected above. Surprisingly, Woodlark and the D'Entrecasteaux have not been identified as the origin of any types of spatula. This could be due to the fact that no substantial collection made in these islands has been located.

Ebony is the preferred wood for spatulas, mortars and pestles. It is durable, carves well and acquires a beautiful patina with use. Blackpalm and other unidentified woods are used less often. Turtleshell, human, cassowary, dugong and whale bone are also regularly used for spatulas, stone occasionally for pestles. One Suau man has been using a dugong tooth as a pestle for most of the twentieth century. Limepots are made from gourds, less often from coconuts. Coconut palm and pandanus leaf is used for baskets.

What has been written above suggests that the following features make a lime spatula valuable: the rarity of its material, the attachments it carries, the quality of its carving, its age and history, including past owners, and the power it has displayed in use with magic.

The above also shows the features characteristic of Massim art. The motifs which occur most frequently on betel-chewing equipment are human or spirit figures, birds, fish, snakes, lizards, flowers and canoes. Some Massim art is two-dimensional, for example, dance paddles and canoe boards. Here, flat, thin boards are covered on one or both sides with low relief carving. Betel-chewing equipment shows that the Massim also have a genius for three-dimensional, sculptural carving. Most representational carving is stylised but a minority of pieces, including some of the finest, are naturalistic. The carvings carry much curvilinear decoration involving many different types of interlocking scrolls. Bands of zigzags are used as dividers and to decorate borders. The older pieces tend to be less decorated than the more recent ones. Usually the incisions on the ebony and blackpalm utensils are filled in with lime which highlights the designs and produces an attractive black and white contrast. The spatulas used by chiefs, people of rank and village leaders carry shell discs, small white cowries or tassels made from shell discs, sections of mother-of-pearl shell and wild banana seeds, but these embellishments have disappeared from most museum pieces.

When Trobrianders meet they chew betel-nuts. Kasaipwalova suggests that the spatulas they display on these occasions symbolise their rank in society and reveal their personality. Properly carved clappers (type 14) and spatulas like that shown in plate 28 are restricted to chiefs and are therefore a sign of their status. Other types of spatula (for example type 23) can be used by anyone. Kasaipwalova suggests someone who uses a spatula with a mortar on its handle may wish to show how practical he is and someone who has a spatula with a complete canoe may be seeking admiration. Narubutau and Kasaipwalova laughed when they saw a photograph of the spatula in plate 96. They said that it displays its owner's ignorance (he does not know how to carve a better one), impatience (he wants one quickly) and pretentiousness (the spatula is too plain to be used by a person of high rank, yet carries chiefly tassels).

Although the production of most types of spatula ceased in the early decades of the twentieth century, there remains much knowledge about them among the Massim. Attempts need to be made to establish what ideological significance the things represented on betel-chewing equipment have. In some cases things may be represented just because they are pretty (for example sea-urchins, spatula type 16). However, Kasaipwalova reports that the handle of the steering oar is a symbol of tenacity and this may account for the carving of some spatulas in imitation of such oars (type 28). It seems clear that other things represented also have an important symbolic significance. What is the significance in Massim culture of the morning star, of snakes, praying mantis, lizards, various types of bird and of the pervasive fish and bird combination? What is the significance of the small being in front of the bigger one in plate 12 and of the long, protruding tongue of the figure in plate 17? We would understand much better how the Massim see themselves, if we had answers to these questions.

96. Spatula with flat, rectangular handle. Wood and tassels consisting of shell discs, wild banana seeds and mother-of-pearl sections, betel-stained. Length 230 mm (9 inches). (Museum für Völkerkunde, Basle, Vb 14095. Photograph: Museum für Völkerkunde, Basle.)

6
Glossary

The words are from the language spoken in Kiriwina, unless indicated otherwise.

Boi: heron.
Bosu: whale or dugong bone lime spatula.
Bulabula: flower represented on lime spatulas and betel-nut pestles.
Ch:aa: lime spatula (Rossel Island).
Gabaela: wooden handle, with crescentic top, to which rows of shell discs are attached, an object of value (Louisiades).
Gesuwali: cassowary bone lime spatula.
Ghena: lime spatula (Tagula).
Kaimili: betel-nut pestle.
Kaipita: betel-nut mortar.
Kauya: envelope-shaped basket.
Kena: lime spatula.
Kenayapu: lime spatula reserved for persons of chiefly rank in the Trobriands.
Kokonu: lime spatula with canoe-tip motif (Rossel Island).
Kula: ceremonial exchange of armshells and shell necklaces in the Massim area. In Kiriwinan the verb *kula* means 'you go'.
Masawa: northern Massim *kula* canoe.
Mwali: shell armband used in *kula* and as an object of wealth.
Nagega: southern Massim *kula* canoe.
Potuma: whale or dugong bone lime spatula (Milne Bay).
Soulava: shell necklace used in *kula* and as an object of wealth.
Tabulabula: lime spatula with flower motif.
Takakupwana: lime spatula of clapper design.
Takubwana: lime spatula with morning star motif.
Takuriga: lime spatula with steering oar motif.
Tanagega: lime spatula with *nagega* canoe motif.
Tanepopo: three-tiered basket.
Taubwara: lime spatula with wild yam motif.
Tiltil: round basket (Wanim Island).
Yaguma: limepot.

7
Museums

United Kingdom
Aberdeen University Anthropological Museum, Marischal College, Aberdeen AB9 1AS. Telephone: 0224 273132. (AUAM)

Cambridge University Museum of Archaeology and Anthropology, Downing Street, Cambridge CB2 3DZ. Telephone: 0223 337733. (UMC)

Horniman Museum, London Road, Forest Hill, London SE23 3PQ. Telephone: 01-699 1872 or 2339 or 4911. (HML)

Liverpool Museum, William Brown Street, Liverpool L3 8EN. Telephone: 051-207 0001 or 5451. (LM)

Museum of Mankind, 6 Burlington Gardens, London W1X 2EX. Telephone: 01-437 2224 or 2227. (MM)

Pitt Rivers Museum, South Parks Road, Oxford OX1 3PP. Telephone: 0865 270927. (PRM)

Royal Museum of Scotland, Chambers Street, Edinburgh EH1 1JF. Telephone: 031-225 7534. (RSM)

Australia
Australian National Gallery, Canberra, ACT 2600. (ANG)

Australian National University, Institute of Anatomy Museum, Canberra, ACT 2600. (IAMC)

Australian Museum, 6-8 College Street, Sydney, New South Wales, 2000. (AMS)

National Museum of Victoria, 285-321 Russell Street, Melbourne, Victoria 3000. (NMV)

Queensland Museum, Cultural Centre, Southbank, Brisbane, Queensland 4000. (QM)

South Australian Museum, North Terrace, Adelaide, South Australia 5006. (SAM)

Austria
Museum für Völkerkunde, Heldenplatz 3, Neue Hofburg, 1010 Vienna 1. (MVV)

France
Musée de l'Homme, Place de Trocadero, 75016 Paris. (MHP)

Germany, East
Museum für Völkerkunde, Täubchenweg 2, 701 Leipzig. (MVL)
Staatliches Museum für Völkerkunde, Japanisches Palais, Karl Marx
    Platz, 806 Dresden. (MVD)

Hungary
Museum of Ethnography, Kossuth Lajos Ter 12, 1055 Budapest.
    (MEB)

Ireland, Republic of
National Museum of Ireland, Kildare Street, Dublin 2. Telephone:
    01-765521. (NMI)

Japan
National Museum of Ethnology, Senri Expo Park, Suita, Osaka.
    (NMEO)

New Zealand
Auckland Institute and Museum, The Domain, Auckland. (AIM)
Otago Museum, Great King Street, Dunedin. (OMD)

Papua New Guinea
National Museum and Art Gallery, Waigani, Port Moresby. (NMPM)

Sweden
Ethnographical Museum of Sweden, Djurgardsbrunnsvägen 34, 5-115
    27 Stockholm. (EMS)

United States of America
Buffalo Museum of Science, Humboldt Parkway, Buffalo, New York
    14211. (BMS)
Field Museum of Natural History, Roosevelt Road at Lake Shore
    Drive, Chicago, Illinois 60605. (FMC)
Robert H. Lowie Museum of Anthropology, 103 Kroeber Hall, Univer-
    sity of California, Berkeley, California 94720. (LMB)
Peabody Museum of Archaeology and Ethnology, 11 Divinity Avenue,
    Cambridge, Massachusetts 02138.

8
Further reading

Publications specially relevant to betel-chewing utensils are indicated with an asterisk.

Abel, Cecil. 'Suau Aesthetics', *Gigibori*, 1 (1974), 34-5.
Beran, Harry. *Massim Tribal Art*. Wollongong City Gallery, 1980.*
Cranstone, B. A. L. *Melanesia: A Short Ethnography*. British Museum, 1961.
Dickson, T. E., and Whitehouse, E. 'An Unusual Ceremonial Lime Spatula from British New Guinea', *Man*, XLII (1942), 49-51.*
Firth, Raymond. *Art and Life in New Guinea*. AMS Press, New York, 1979.
Fortune, R. F. *Sorcerers of Dobu*. Dutton, New York, 1963.
Germer, Ernst. 'Kalkspatel aus dem Massim-Gebiet, New Guinea', *Abhandlungen und Berichte des Staatlichen Museums für Völkerkunde Dresden*, 30 (1965), 123-39.*
Haddon, A. C. *The Decorative Art of British New Guinea*. Academy House, Dublin, 1894.*
Jenness, D., and Ballantyne, A. *The Northern D'Entrecasteaux*. Clarendon Press, Oxford, 1920.
Jüptner, H. 'Über das Betelnusskauen auf den Trobriand Inseln', *Baessler-Archiv*, Neue Folge, XVII (1969), 371-86.*
Krenger, W. 'Über die Wirkung des Betels', *Ciba Zeitschrift*, 7 (1942), 2942-7.
Lawson, Lisa. *Music from the D'Entrecasteaux Islands*. National Arts School, Papua New Guinea, 1983.
Leach, Jerry W., and Leach, Edmund (editors). *The Kula*. Cambridge University Press, 1983.
Malinowski, Bronislaw. *Typescript*. Museum of Mankind, Archives Ethnographic Document 1009, not dated.
Malinowski, Bronislaw. *Argonauts of the Western Pacific*. Routledge and Kegan Paul, London, 1966.
Malinowski, Bronislaw. *Coral Gardens and their Magic*, volume 1. Dover Publications, New York, 1978.
Malinowski, Bronislaw. *The Sexual Life of Savages in North Western Melanesia*. Routledge and Kegan Paul, London, 1982.
Newton, Douglas. *Massim*. Museum of Primitive Art, New York, 1975.*
Schlesier, Erhard. *Eine ethnographische Sammlung aus Südost-Neuguinea*. Edition Herodot, Göttingen, 1986.*

Seligman, C. G. 'Lime Spatulae from Rossel Island, British New Guinea', *Man*, XVI (1916), 6-7.*

Seligman, C. G. *The Melanesians of British New Guinea*. Cambridge University Press, 1910.

Shack, William A. *The Kula. A Bronislaw Malinowski Centennial Exhibition*. Lowie Museum, Berkeley, 1985.

Vargyas, Gabor. 'Lime Spatulae from the Massim Area of South-East New Guinea in the Ethnographical Museum, Budapest', *Acta Ethnographica Academiae Scientiarum Hungaricae*, 29 (1980), 427-62.*

Webster, W. D. *Catalogues of Ethnological Specimens*. Bicester, 1890s-1900s.*

Index

Page numbers in italic refer to illustrations